# Princess Palace

**Have fun completing the activities in this book!**

Press out and decorate the bookmarks, postcards, door hangers, models, and cards.

You can use your puffy stickers to finish the press-out pieces, on the book pages, or anywhere else you like. Once you've removed the stickers, you can use the cover as a frame to display your favorite pictures.

# How to use your press-out pieces:

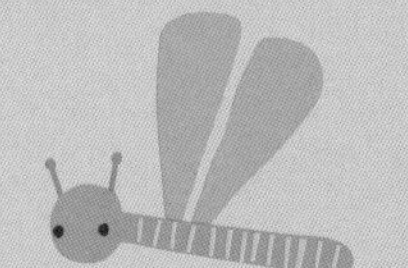

**At the back of the book, there are fun press outs for you to decorate, display, or give away.**

1. Pull out the card pages at the back of the book.

Princess door hanger

Press out and decorate the door hanger.

MY ROOM

2. Gently push the shapes until they pop out.

3. Complete the press-out pieces using doodles, color, and your puffy stickers.

# Perfect palace

Color the palace.

Circle the princess that is different.

# Tiara tangle

Draw lines to match each princess to the correct colored tiara.

Color the crown.

# Trace and see

Trace the lines to see who's in the field. Then add color and draw a face!

Color more flowers in the field.

Shoe search
Find and circle
the princess's shoe.

# Princess panic

Guide the princess through the maze to reach the palace.

# Find the difference

Circle five differences between the scenes.

# Royal word search

Find the words.

Words can go across or down.

crown

pony

palace

queen

jewel

| | | | | | | |
|---|---|---|---|---|---|---|
| p | s | g | t | i | j | h |
| o | j | e | w | e | l | c |
| n | m | b | n | o | w | v |
| y | c | r | o | w | n | y |
| k | s | d | t | c | x | b |
| l | p | a | l | a | c | e |
| a | b | q | u | e | e | n |

Under the sea
Color the underwater palace.

Look at the picture and check the boxes when you find the things on the list.
1 treasure chest
2 pink fish
3 flags
How many crowns can you see?

# Tasty treats

Draw lines to match the sweet pairs.

Princess Carla's collections
Circle the one that doesn't match in each collection.

Help the princess to trace the words.

dress

pony

tiara

# Copy and color

Color the picture to make it match.

# Jewel maze

Guide the prince through the maze to reach the princess.

# Gorgeous gems

Trace the lines to finish the beautiful gems, then add color.

Color the necklace.

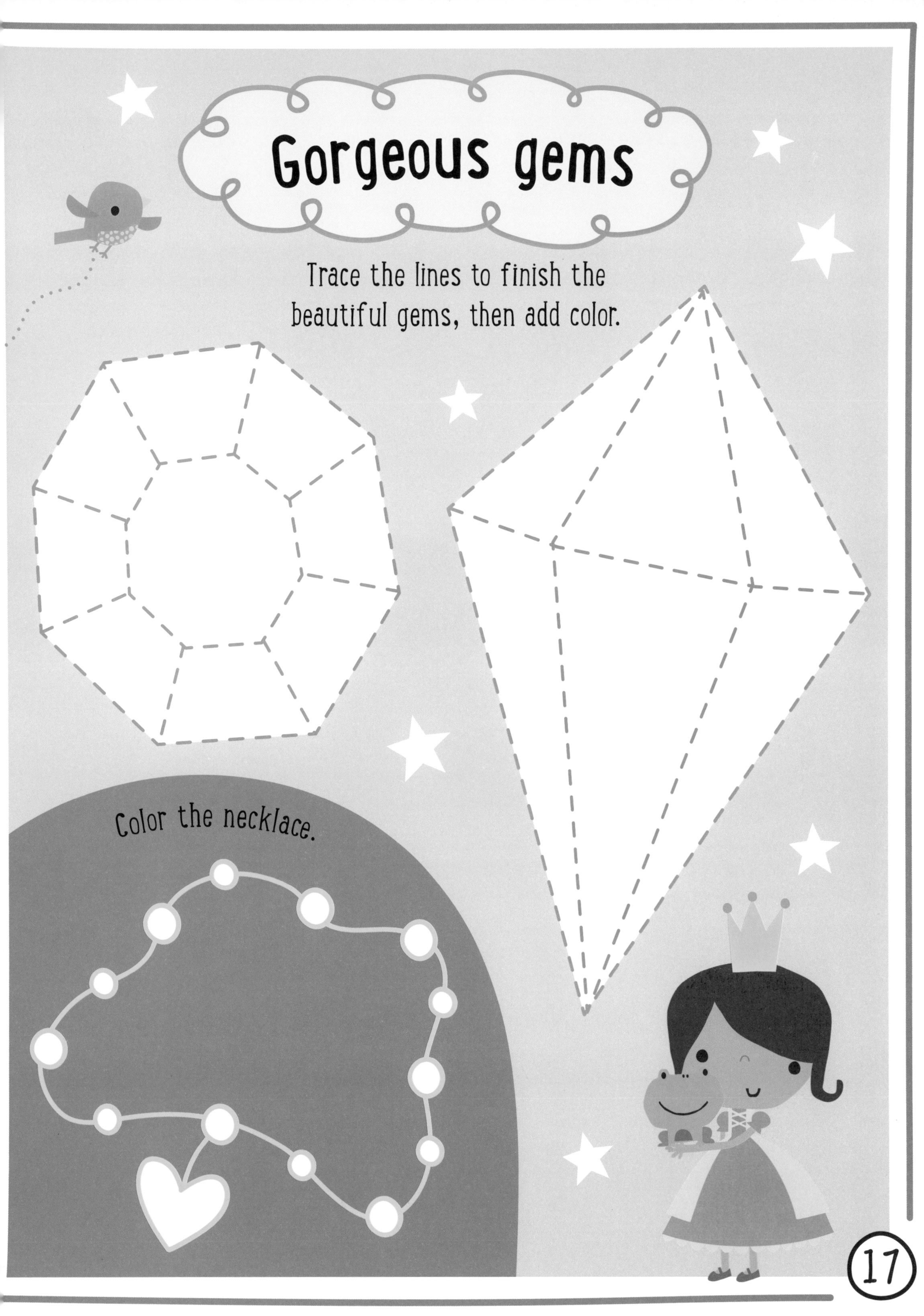

# Palace gardens

Color the palace and design a flag.

How many butterflies
can you see?
Trace their trails!
Color
the flowers.

# Princess fun

Follow the lines to see where the princess is going.

tower

horseback riding

forest

palace

Beautiful bedroom
Color the bed.
Circle three tiaras.
a
b
c
d
e
Decorate the slippers.

# Spelling bee

Help the bee to trace the words.

palace

queen

Copy the crown. Use the grid to help you.

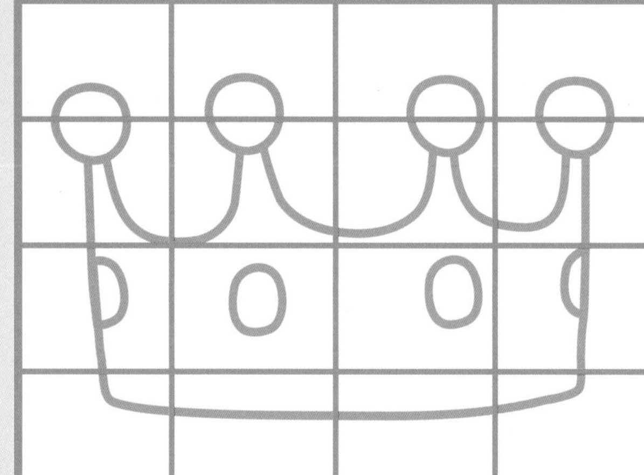

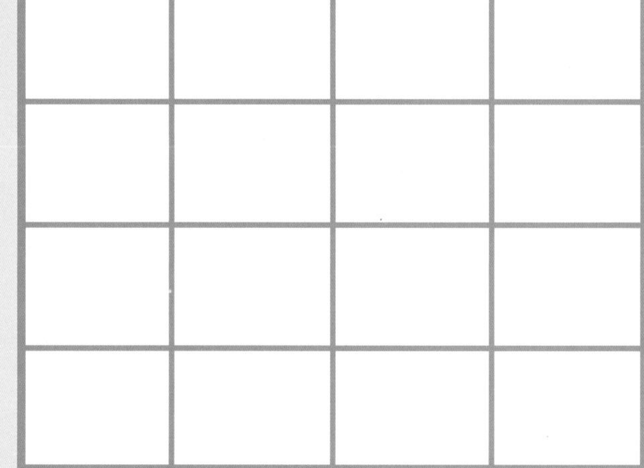

# Playful pup

Find and circle the princess's puppy.

Jewel forest
How many birds
can you see?

Look at the picture and check the boxes when you find the things on the list.
2 pink jewels
1 purple jewel
3 green jewels
Color the princess.
Draw more toadstools in the forest.

# Royal banquet

Read the chef's list and circle the items on the shelves.

Color the chef's hat.

Circle the lollipop that doesn't match.

Palace dancers
Trace the lines to finish the dancers.
27

# Castle creator

Color and doodle to finish the castle.

# Fantastic flags

Color and decorate the flags.

Circle the princess that is different.

Color by numbers
Use the key to color the picture.
6
4
6
5
1
5
5
1
5
1
1
1
1
2
2
1
1
2
2
1 = pink
2 = purple
3 = yellow
4 = blue
5 = orange
6 = red

# Time for tea

Color
the teacups.
Fill the stand
with cupcakes.
Circle the cake that is different.

# Belle of the ball

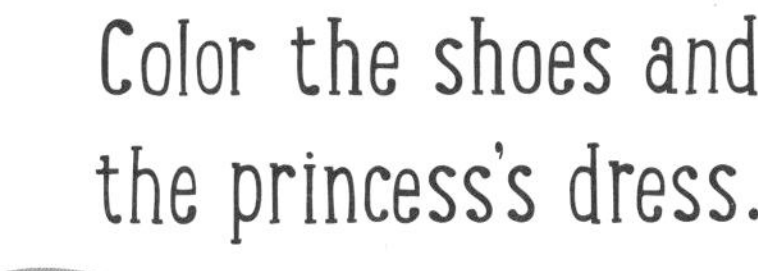

Color the shoes and the princess's dress.

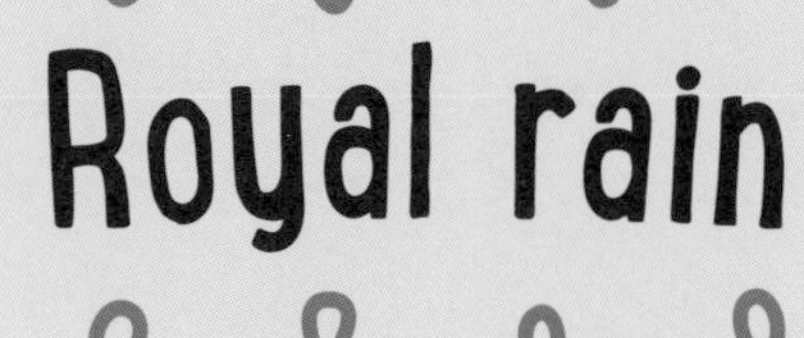

# Royal rain

The princesses are playing in the rain!

Draw faces on the rain clouds.

Color the jewels on the umbrellas.

Decorate the raincoats.

# In the greenhouse

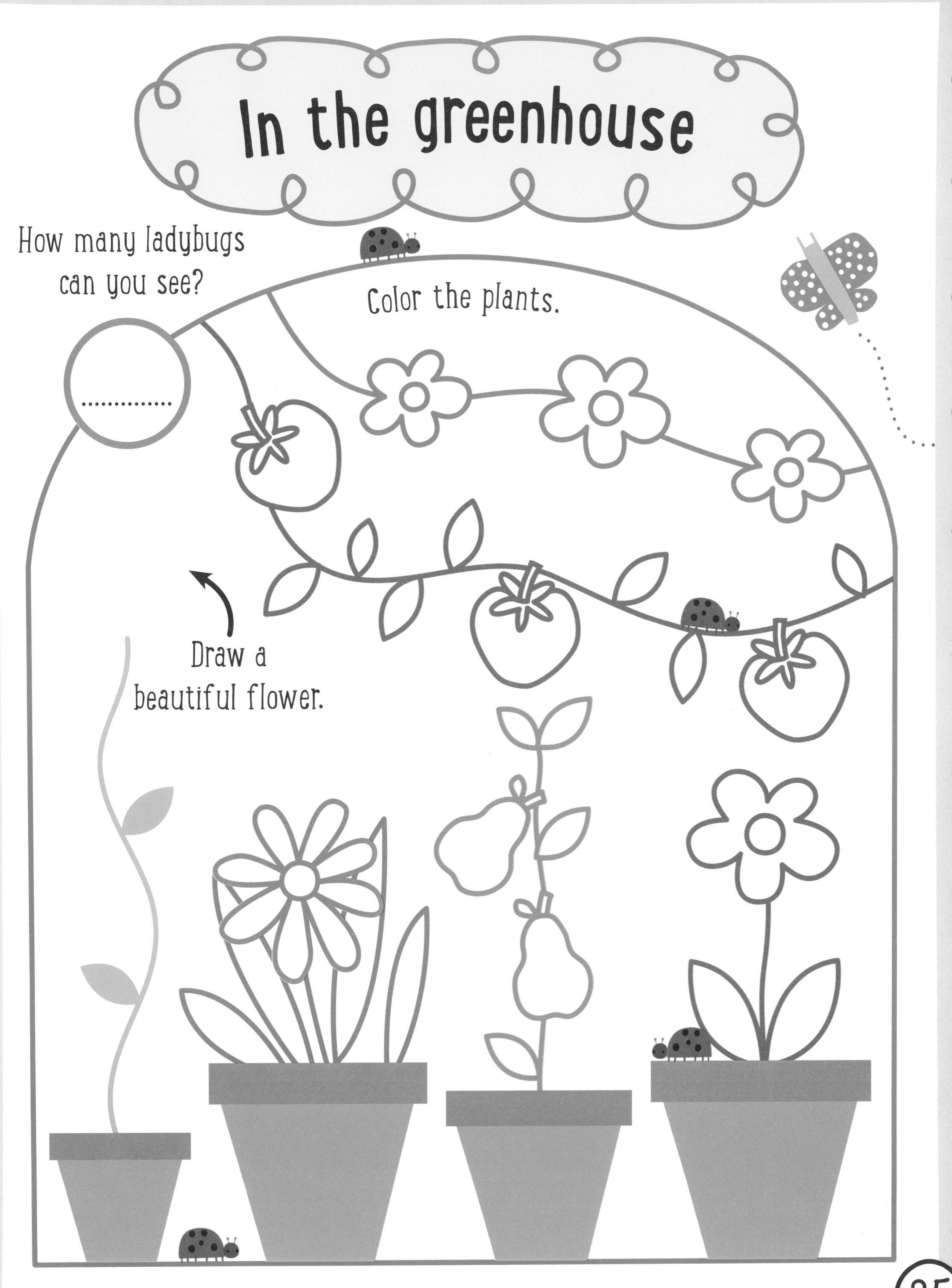

Winter wonderland
Give the snowman
a sparkling crown.
Decorate the coat
for the princess.

Decorate
the mittens.
How many snowflakes
can you see?
Copy the winter palace. Use the grid to help you.

# Brilliant bakes

Decorate the cookies.

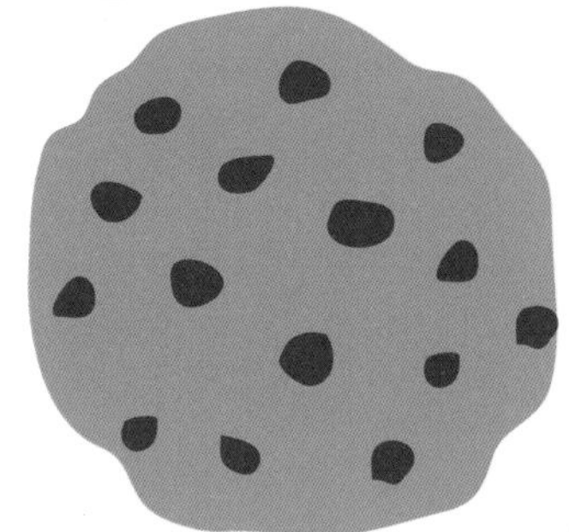

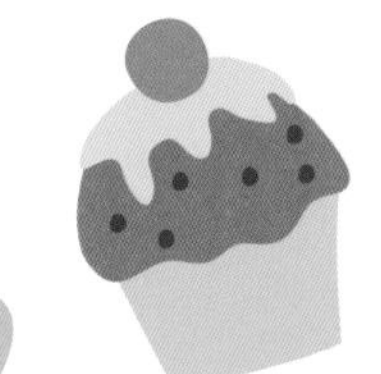

Check the boxes to design your perfect cake.

- ☐ pink frosting
- ☐ white frosting
- ☐ chocolate sprinkles
- ☐ candies
- ☐ cherries

Now draw your cake here.

# Cool kites

Color the kites.

Follow the strings to see which kite the princess is flying.

# Field friends

Trace the lines to see who's in the field.

Circle the apple that is different.

# Time to trace

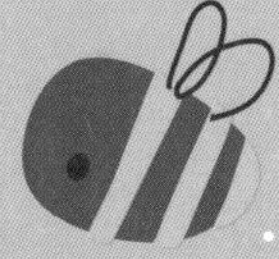

Help the princess to trace the words.

pony

hay

apple

ride

# Princess party

Color the bunting.

Draw more balloons.

How many cupcakes can you see?
Color the picture to make it match.

# Pony maze

Guide the pony through the maze to reach the stable.

# Stunning sunflowers

The princesses are having a gardening competition.

Circle the tallest sunflower and color the trophy.

# Royal ball

Decorate the gowns.

Color
the invitation.

# Crown town

The princess is crown shopping!
Draw more crowns on the shelves.

How many blue jewels can you count? ..........

# Royal rose garden

Color the roses and add leaves to the stems.

Draw your own rose.

Color
the shed.

# Fill the frames

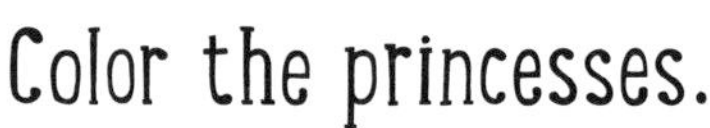

Color the princesses.

Draw yourself as a princess.

# Perfect picnic

Trace the lines to see what the princesses are having for their picnic.

Decorate the picnic quilt.

# High in the sky

Decorate the hot-air balloons.

Circle three carriages.

Copy the hot-air balloon. Use the grid to help you.

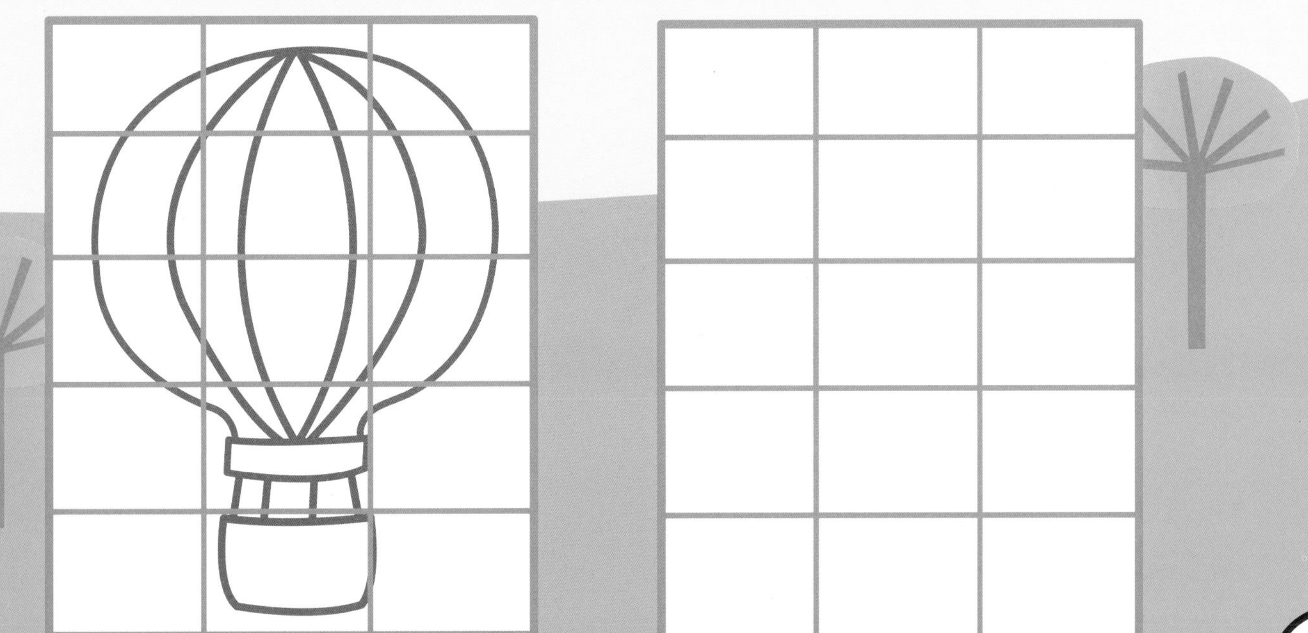

# Enchanted forest

Draw lines to match the pairs.

Draw cupcakes on the path.

# Beautiful birds

The princess is feeding the birds!

Color the birdhouses.

Color the birds.

# Color by numbers

Use the key to color the picture.

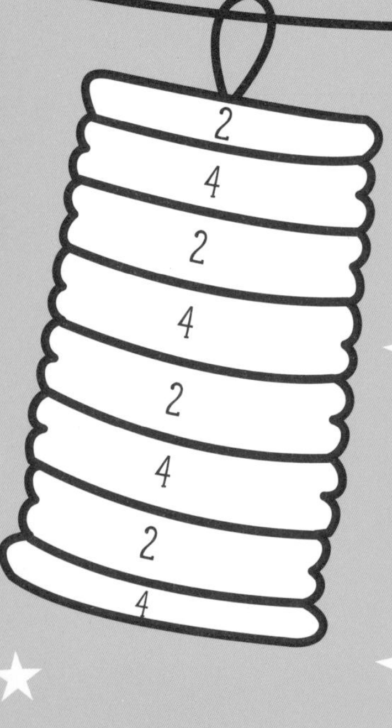

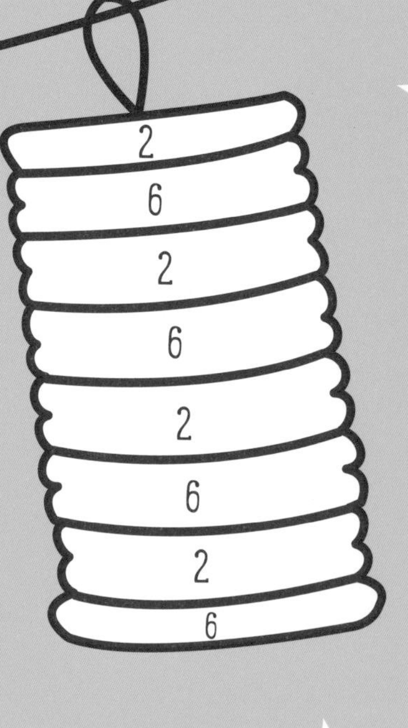


| | | |
|---|---|---|
| 1 = pink | 2 = purple | 3 = yellow |
| 4 = blue | 5 = orange | 6 = red |

# Find the difference

Circle five differences between the scenes.

# Take the lead!

Follow the tangled leads to see which puppy belongs to the princess.

Tasty treat
Trace the trails to find out which princess gets the cake.
Color the cake.

# Glorious gowns

Color and decorate the gowns for the princess.

# Crown maze

Guide the princess through the maze to reach the crown.

# Treasure word search

Find the words.
Words can go across or down.

gem

gold

ruby

silver

shine

| | | | | | | |
|---|---|---|---|---|---|---|
| b | r | k | g | m | n | o |
| g | e | m | o | n | a | t |
| l | s | i | l | v | e | r |
| k | h | x | d | k | o | u |
| q | i | v | x | z | i | b |
| v | n | r | a | m | j | y |
| f | e | h | s | b | r | c |

# Masked ball

The princesses are going to a masked ball!
Decorate the masks.

# Make your mark!

Press out and decorate the bookmarks.

Add your own doodles.

# Princess door hanger

Press out and decorate the door hanger.

MY ROOM

# Mini mail

Press out and complete the postcards, then give them to your friends!

# Perfect press outs

Press out the princesses, then fold along the crease to make them stand up.

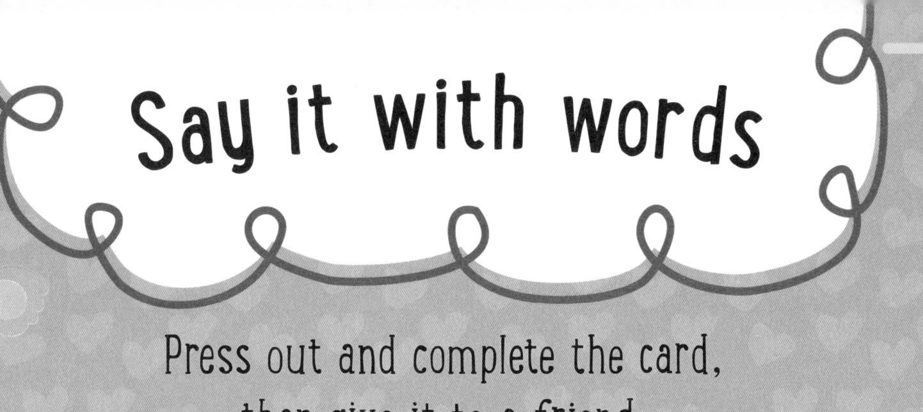

# Say it with words

Press out and complete the card,
then give it to a friend.

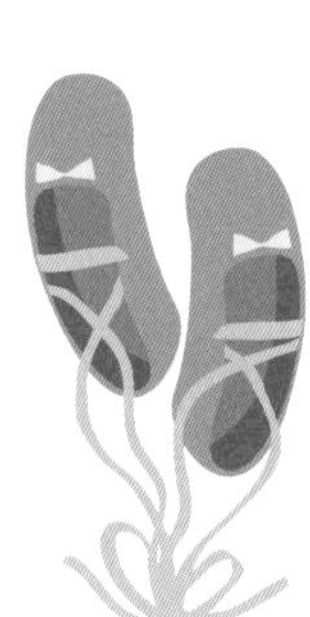

# Make your mark!

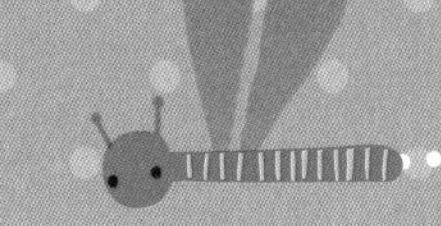

Press out and decorate the bookmarks.

Add your own doodles.

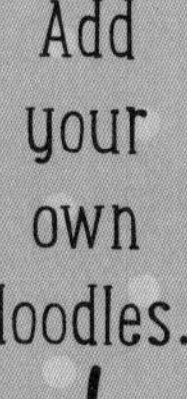

Press out and decorate the door hanger.

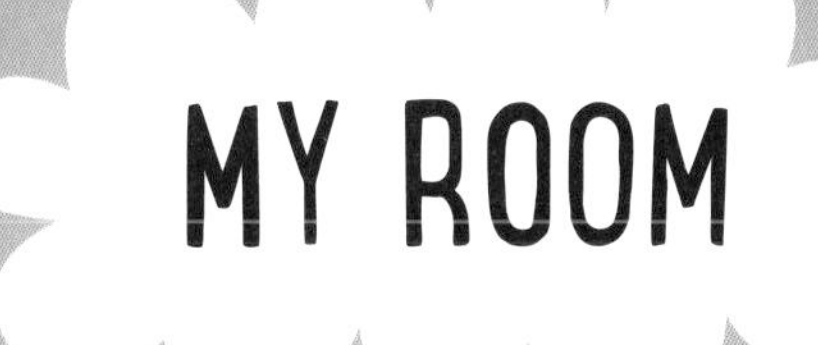

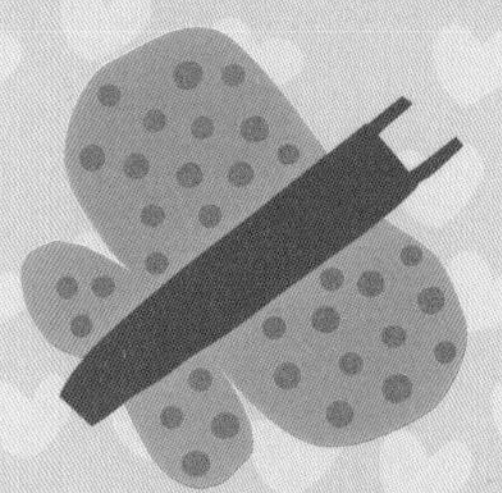

# Mini mail

Press out and complete the postcards, then give them to your friends!

# Perfect press outs

Press out the prince and princess, then fold along the crease to make them stand up.

Press out and complete the card,
then give it to a friend.

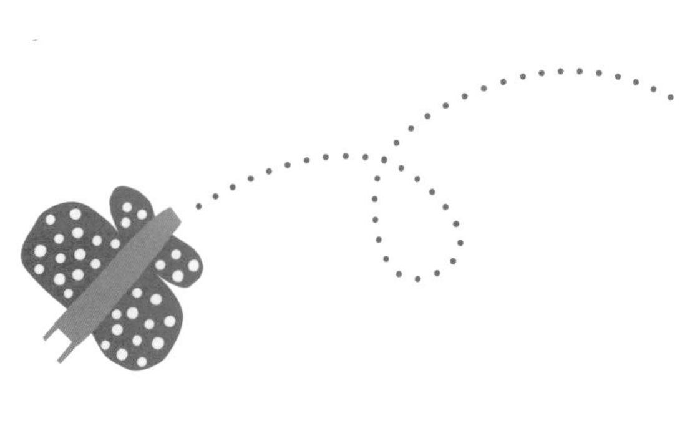